Contents

Words appearing in the text in bold, **like this**, are explained in the glossary.

Chapter 1

An exciting and worthwhile career

So, you are thinking about joining the armed forces or the civilian forces. Is it the life of action and possible danger that attracts you? Or does the opportunity to serve your country or community appeal to you? Serving in the armed or civilian forces will certainly involve both of these.

What are the armed and civilian forces?

The armed forces – the Army, the Royal Navy, and the Royal Air Force (RAF) – protect the security of the United Kingdom. They defend the nation from attack and protect its interests abroad. They also take part in international peace-keeping and disaster relief. The Army operates mainly on land, the Navy at sea, and the RAF in the air. The civilian forces include the police, the fire and rescue service, **customs and excise**, and the prison service. Their role is to protect the security of the community.

below: *Being a soldier requires a lot of commitment and physical effort.*

It takes more than courage

To work in the armed or civilian forces you need to be fit and healthy. You must be able to accept discipline and obey rules and orders. But, don't worry – your basic training will help you to develop these abilities. It will also give you the confidence and knowledge to use your **initiative** and take split-second decisions. Everyone in the forces works with a team of highly trained people, so you need to be able to get on well with others.

above: *This policewoman is on patrol.*

Still interested? Read on...

The next few pages give you some basic information. They tell you about some of the conditions of work shared by all of the forces and whether you are eligible to apply. Each chapter then looks at a particular force. It tells you the qualifications you need to join at different levels and how to apply to join. It describes the basic training and the range of jobs available in each force. Then, at the end of the book, there are tips on how to present yourself well in an interview, examples of jobs in the armed forces, and where to find out more information.

HOW THE NUMBERS COMPARE

Force	Approximate number employed	Approximate starting salary
Army	109,000	£14,000
Royal Air Force	52,000	£14,500
Royal Navy	39,500	£12,000
Police	140,000	£20,000
Fire and Rescue service	39,000	£19,500
HM Prisons	47,000	£17,500

Conditions of work

Conditions of work include the time you are expected to start in the morning and the number of hours you work a day. They also cover the place where you work, the nature of your job, and things such as holidays. Fighting a war and protecting the nation or the community involves a particular set of conditions of work. Your hours of work, what you wear, and how much you are trained will be different from other jobs.

Irregular hours

When you join one of the armed or civilian forces do not expect your hours to be like those of your friends who are working in a nine-to-five office job. Instead you will often have to work in shifts and at weekends. You will sometimes be working in the evening and sometimes at night. If you work for the police or fire service, you may be called out to an emergency at any time. Most soldiers, however, work from 8 a.m. until 5 p.m. and have every weekend off, but not, of course, when they are on **operations**.

below: *Fire-fighting is dangerous work, but training helps to reduce the danger.*

Uniform and training

All the armed and civilian forces provide uniforms, which you must wear when you are on duty. You are expected to be neat and smart. Much of the work of the forces is out of doors and so the purpose of the uniform is to be practical as well as to identify you as a member of the force.

Whichever force you join, you will receive a thorough basic training. Further training continues throughout your career and many of the skills you learn will help you find a job when you leave the force.

Commitment

Both the armed forces and the civilian forces are looking for people who are committed to their jobs. The armed forces expect you to sign up for several years, although you can leave at the end of basic training if you change your mind. After that, you need to give a year's notice if you want to leave the Army.

EQUAL OPPORTUNITIES

All the armed and civilian forces have an equal opportunities policy – they are committed to employing women and men from all religions and ethnic groups.

OTHER BENEFITS

Pay: salaries are usually higher than for similar jobs in commercial companies.
Meals: food is usually provided and is cheaper than you would normally buy elsewhere.
Accommodation: housing is provided in the armed forces, although you can choose to live off the base.
Travel: in the armed forces you will have the opportunity to travel to many different parts of the world.

Are the armed forces right for you?

The armed forces accept a wide range of people and skills. The better your exam results, the more choice you will have in careers, but the main thing the armed forces are looking for is the right kind of person.

Personal qualities

To enjoy the armed forces and do well in them, you need to have the right attitude. You will be expected to do your best and to do it willingly. You will need to be well organized and self-disciplined and able to accept orders from others. At the same time you should be self-confident enough to think for yourself and to act quickly.

Physical qualities

You need to be physically fit and healthy to join the armed forces. Not all health conditions disqualify you from joining, so if you have a health condition, you should discuss it with someone at the recruitment centre. A large part of basic training is spent increasing your fitness, and the fitter you are before you start, the easier you will find it. Look at the "Get ahead!" box on page 11 for ways to increase your fitness.

above: *These soldiers are wearing special desert kit.*

Equal opportunities

The armed forces treat everyone equally, whatever their gender, religion or ethnic background. Vegetarian, **halal**, and **kosher** food can be provided, even on exercises and operations. Women play an important part in the forces, although there are some things that women are not allowed to do, such as fighting as soldiers on the **front line** or serving in submarines.

Sport and adventure

If you are good at sport, the armed forces give you a fantastic opportunity to develop your abilities, right up to Olympic standard. You can play football, rugby, basketball, hockey, and other sports. You can take up adventure challenges involving water sports, snow sports, mountaineering, and similar activities, and you will be sent on challenging training exercises in many parts of the world.

ARE YOU ELIGIBLE?

Age: you must be at least 16 years old to join up.
Nationality: you must have been a citizen of the United Kingdom or a Commonwealth country or the Republic of Ireland.
Academic qualifications: you can join with GCSEs, S-levels or no qualifications at all, but to join as an officer you need to have five GCSEs/S-grades including English and Maths, and the equivalent of three A-levels or three Highers.

above: *Working in the forces can often mean a posting to an exciting environment in a different country.*

Chapter 2

The British Army

The Army fulfils many roles. Apart from training exercises and fighting, its soldiers are often called upon to keep the peace in war-torn countries and to deliver aid to areas hit by an earthquake or other disaster. Such a complex organization involves different jobs, many of them similar to those in civilian organizations.

The Army groups its careers into seven main areas: combat; engineering; **logistics**; IT and communications; human resources, administration and finance; healthcare; and specialist jobs. For more about the jobs in each group see page 49.

ARMY WORDS

The Army is divided into different groupings and sub-groupings. A corps is associated with a particular job, such as the Royal Army Medical Corps or the Intelligence Corps. A battalion is a group of infantry soldiers or engineers. A **regiment** consists of one or two battalions. A brigade is a large group that includes several regiments and battalions.

Helping you decide

How can you tell which career to go for? An Armed Forces Careers Office (AFCO) will help – you can find the address of your nearest one in the telephone directory. You can talk to a recruitment advisor there and watch a video about the Army before you do the Army Entrance Test.

left: *Cadets are allowed to fire rifles under the supervision of an army sergeant at an Army Cadet Force annual camp.*

This test is done on a computer and your score will help the recruitment advisor tell you which careers are likely to suit you. You can also spend two days at an Army Selection Camp. There you can talk to recruits going through the basic training and get a real feel for Army life.

Applying to join

If you decide to apply, you will need to fill out an application form and be interviewed by an officer. The more effort you have made to find out about the Army, the better your interview is likely to go. You will also be given a medical examination, an **aptitude test**, and a physical fitness test. Only after all this do you finally decide if you want to sign up and join the Army.

Get ahead!

You can increase your fitness by working out every day. Running, press-ups, and sit-ups are the best ways of increasing your fitness. Start off by working out for about 20 minutes a day and increase it gradually. Make sure that you warm up before you work out and cool down afterwards. The physical fitness test will include a 2.4-km (1.5-mile) run. If you are male, you should aim to run this in less than 12 minutes and 20 seconds; if you are female, you should run this in less than 14 minutes and 35 seconds.

left: *Working out in a gym and running uphill will help you get fit.*

Basic training

Whatever career you follow, your life in the Army begins with basic training. Once you have passed Recruit Selection and joined up you will spend the first 12 weeks at an Army training camp. By the end of it, you will be physically much fitter and you will have learnt all the basic skills of handling weapons as well as first aid, map reading, and camouflage. You will probably be more confident and have made many good friends.

Fitness

As you progress through basic training you will become increasingly fit and more and more will be required of you. This is a real challenge, but if you begin to flag, your sergeant will be there to urge you on! By the end, you will be amazed at what you can achieve, including running with a heavy pack on your back. But it's not all hard work. You will also find yourself abseiling, kayaking, and taking part in other adventurous activities.

Get ahead!

Inspection tests check how tidy you keep yourself and your belongings. Get used to keeping your clothes clean and neat. Learn how to use an iron!

Discipline and initiative

The Army needs its soldiers to obey orders without question sometimes, but at the same time, soldiers have to be able to think for themselves and use their initiative. Sounds contradictory? It will all become clear during training. Knowing what you are doing and what is expected of you at all times is the key to success.

The next stage – specialist training

After basic training you have a few days off before you join your regiment and begin Phase 2 specialist training. Phase 2 training equips you for the particular career you have chosen in the Army. It may last a few weeks or up to 2 years.

BASIC TRAINING – THE LOWDOWN

Week	What happens
1	**Drill** practice, map-reading, first aid, and handling a rifle
2	Your first exercise, **fieldcraft** and night training, including camouflage techniques and building shelters
3	Computer-simulated rifle range – a bit like computer games but more real
4	Target practice on the live-firing range
5	Tests to prove your physical fitness, including a 2.4-kilometre (1.5-mile) run, and drill tests
6	A long weekend on home leave
7	Getting to grips with an obstacle course that includes a 3.5-metre (12-foot) wall and a river rope swing
8	Your second exercise, including live fire
9	Fitness test that includes a 6-mile march in full combat gear
10	Adventurous training, for example abseiling or canoeing
11	Test week in which you are assessed by a Section Commander
12	Final parade – called "passing out" – with your family and friends there to applaud you.

below: *This officer is leading recruits during basic training.*

Training for life

Every job the Army offers is a vital one. In Phase 2 training you learn the skills needed for the career you have chosen – skills that will give you one or more qualifications that will help you get a job when you leave the Army. If you work hard and do well, you will be given more responsibility and **promotion**.

Combat

Combat troops make up the largest group in the Army and include infantry soldiers, gunners, tank crew, and parachutists. Combat troops are trained not only to fight in different **terrains**, from jungles to deserts, they are also called on to deliver aid in disaster areas and for peace-keeping in war-torn countries.

Combat support

There are many job areas in combat support. Engineering covers a wide range of jobs from building bridges to laying mines and demolition. Engineering jobs include brick-laying and vehicle maintenance as well as mechanical and electrical engineering. The Army needs a constant supply of food, ammunition, and other goods, and it is the job of those who work in logistics to supply them. Sometimes delivery is by truck, at other times by helicopter drop or motorcycle.

below: *Working in combat support is a specialized job in the Army.*

above: *Army medical teams work in the field as well as in army hospitals.*

Receiving up-to-date information is as essential for a **platoon** of soldiers as it is for those planning the larger operation. Providing information is the job of IT and communications and includes signals and military intelligence.

Services

No part of the Army would run smoothly without the Adjutant General's Corps. It trains soldiers to be military clerks in administration, human resources, and finance. Other specialist jobs include doctors, dentists, nurses, dog trainers, military police, and musicians. The table on page 49 gives a few examples of the many jobs available in each career group. Most of the technical jobs in the Army require a GCSE in Maths and many also require Science and English. Grade D is the minimum but higher is better.

CASE STUDY

Michael is a fusilier in the Royal Regiment of Fusiliers.

I joined the Army when I was 18 because, although I had quite good GCSEs, my life was going nowhere. I was out of work, living on my own, and I thought the Army would give me some stability. Basic training was challenging. You have to be determined to get through it, but you're all in it together and help each other. You get an amazing sense of achievement when you complete it!

After basic training, I did advanced infantry training and my battalion is currently stationed in Cyprus. I'm 24 now and intend to stay in the Army – I feel I've grown up a lot and I see the world from a different perspective.

Officers

To be an officer in the armed forces you need to be a good leader. This means that you can communicate well with the soldiers you command. You have to be able to think clearly in difficult situations and make decisions quickly. You also need to relay those decisions clearly and quickly and give your soldiers the information they need to do their jobs.

Being an officer means that you need to win the trust and respect of your soldiers and, in turn, to trust and respect them. Officer training helps you acquire these qualities. You can choose one of three different routes to becoming an officer.

Commissioned officers

A **commissioned officer** is someone who commands other soldiers. Cadets aiming to become commissioned officers train at the Royal Military Academy Sandhurst in Surrey for 11 months. The training is designed to improve physical fitness and mental alertness. It includes learning about the Army and military tactics as well as how to use a rifle and survive in the field. Personal appearance is important and drills encourage teamwork and discipline.

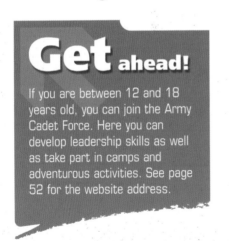

Get ahead!

If you are between 12 and 18 years old, you can join the Army Cadet Force. Here you can develop leadership skills as well as take part in camps and adventurous activities. See page 52 for the website address.

At the end of the first term, officer cadets take part in a week's adventurous training. There are various challenging options including skiing, kayaking, and free-fall. At the end of the second term, cadets go on an adventurous training expedition (which could be in Britain or abroad) that puts all that they have learned to the test. After Sandhurst, commissioned officers train for the particular regiment they have chosen.

Professionally qualified officers

People with professional qualifications, such as lawyers, doctors, nurses, lawyers, and vets, also train at Sandhurst but their training is much shorter – just 4 weeks. During this time they improve their physical fitness and learn how to handle a weapon as well as basic military and fieldcraft skills, such as map-reading, first aid, and maintaining a vehicle.

Non-commissioned officers

You don't have to join the army as an officer cadet to become an officer. **Non-commissioned officers** (NCOs) are soldiers who have worked their way up through the ranks. Anyone who shows leadership potential will be encouraged and promoted. Some may go to Sandhurst as a Late Entry commission; others will take part in the Army's Command, Leadership and Management programme.

below: *These officer cadets are on their passing out parade at Sandhurst.*

Chapter 3

Royal Air Force

The Royal Air Force (also known as the RAF) defends the skies above Britain. It joins with other armed forces to protect British interests abroad and to bring peace to trouble spots around the world. Aircrews may also be called on to deliver aid to people left **destitute** by war or natural disasters, while helicopter crews are always on stand-by to rescue people in trouble in the mountains and on the seas around our coasts.

below: *The Eurofighter Typoon is one of the modern fighter aircraft.*

Career groups

Fighters, **reconnaissance**, and transport aircraft are the core of the RAF. Some of them are listed in the box opposite. The aircrews are the front-line forces in the air and they are supported on the ground by an array of trades – engineers, technicians, air traffic controllers, and flight operators. Yet other trades – catering, medical, personnel, and administrative staff – service the whole organization.

The RAF has its own regiment of soldiers too – gunners who defend air bases at home and abroad. You can find out more about these different careers on pages 22 and 23 and from any Armed Forces Careers Office (AFCO). Look in your local telephone directory to find the address of your nearest AFCO.

The selection process

The first step is to contact your nearest AFCO to get an information pack to help you decide which career you are interested in. You can also talk to a member of staff at AFCO who will answer your questions.

You will then fill in an application form and sit aptitude tests to see whether the career you have chosen is right for you. Then you will be interviewed. The interviewer wants to find out what sort of person you are and why you have chosen the career you have. The interview is followed by a fitness test, a medical test, and a final interview. If you want to join as an officer or aircrew, you will have to spend a few days at RAF Cranwell in Lincolnshire. All being well, you will then be given a formal offer of service. The whole selection process can take between 5 and 18 months.

above: *Part of the RAF's job is to rescue people in difficulty in remote parts of the UK and at sea.*

KNOW YOUR PLANES

Aircraft	Main use	No. in crew
Harrier jumpjet	fighter, air support for ground troops, flying from aircraft carriers, reconnaissance	1 or 2
Eurofighter Typhoon	fighter	1 or 2
Tornado GR4	bomber	2
Sentry	surveillance and airborne control centre	17
Nimrod	reconnaissance, search and rescue	13
Tornado GR4A	reconnaissance	2
Hercules	transport and troop carrier	3
Chinook helicopter	transport	2 to 4
Sea King helicopter	transport and search and rescue	4

Training in the RAF

Being selected and accepted as a recruit is an achievement in itself. It means that you have the potential to be self-disciplined, take responsibility, and play your part in a fast-moving, high-tech organization. Training helps you to realize those potentials. It also makes you more physically and mentally fit than you may have thought possible.

The training you do depends on whether you intend to join an RAF trade, become a non-commissioned member of an aircrew (NCA) or become an officer. Whichever route you take you will start with several weeks of military training.

Military training

All trades and NCA go first to RAF Halton in Buckinghamshire for 9 weeks of military training. Here you learn about the different aircraft and what they do. You will learn how to handle a rifle and to obey orders on parade-ground drills. At the same time you will become physically fitter as you meet ever greater challenges.

Trade training

Trade training begins at a number of RAF stations and can take up to 18 months. You will be posted to an RAF training station where you will learn your chosen trade from the experts. Worried about qualifications? Don't be. Different trades require different qualifications, from none through to GCSEs or S-grades to A-levels or Highers. You can find more about the qualifications needed for some of the trades on page 50. Furthermore, trade training gives you **National Vocational Qualification** (NVQ) or Modern Apprenticeship qualifications that will help you get a job when you leave the RAF.

NCA

Non-commissioned aircrew (NCA) are people whose job involves flying but who are not officers. After military training at RAF Halton, NCA go to RAF Cranwell in Lincolnshire for 10 weeks, during which time they learn about leadership, become more self-confident and able to take responsibility. The training involves a challenging field exercise that allows you to put into practice everything you have learnt. This is followed by training in the particular kind of weapons systems you will operate. You may, for example, learn how to use **radar** and **sonar** equipment to monitor ships.

Officers

Officers work throughout the RAF. All pilots are officers and are in charge of their aircrew. Elsewhere, officers lead teams of trades people, whole **squadrons**, right up to running the whole service. To join as an officer you need to have A-levels, Highers or a university degree. Training takes place at RAF Cranwell and lasts 24 weeks. It will test your physical fitness and includes military and leadership training.

below: *Hose running is part of the Defence Fire Service training at RAF Odiham.*

above: *These RAF pilots are flying a rescue helicopter over mountainous terrain.*

Careers for life

The RAF offers a wide range of careers, which all qualify you for similar work when you leave the service. Most aircraft are crewed by just one or two people, but all of them are supported on the ground by engineers, telecommunications experts, administrators, caterers, health workers, and so on. People who work hard get plenty of opportunity for further training and promotion. They will leave the RAF with qualifications – from NVQs to university degrees – that are recognized by commercial companies.

Aircrew

After training, pilots may find themselves flying supersonic jets, large transport planes or helicopters. Whatever plane they fly they will leave with the skills required to fly commercial aircraft or helicopters or become a pilot trainer. Weapons systems include missiles, radar, radio, and systems that hunt for submarines or monitor ships. Weapons systems operators also include those who operate the winch in a rescue helicopter and those who look after troops on a transport plane. Weapons systems operators gain special skills in, for example, telecommunications or foreign languages.

Engineering and IT

If you are technically minded, you will find plenty of scope in the RAF. There are two large groups of engineers: **avionics** engineers maintain the aircraft and all the on-board systems and general technicians look after all the machinery and systems used on the ground.

People who work in Air Operations use the latest IT and communications systems to produce flight plans and control air traffic. They know exactly where each aircraft is at any time. Communications specialists operate and maintain equipment such as radar and radio aerials and antennae. Intelligence analysts monitor, collect, and analyse information on other forces.

Administration and others

Managing and running the day-to-day activities of the RAF is a major challenge. Spare parts have to be supplied, equipment has to be transported from one place to another and accounted for, thousands of hungry mouths have to be fed. The organization uses all the same skills and careers as companies to look after their finances and their staff. But not many companies also employ musicians, photographers, and sports trainers, let alone their own police force and regiment. The RAF does!

CASE STUDY

Phil is a chief technician in the RAF.

I hadn't thought about the RAF until I went to an AFCO with a friend who was thinking of joining up. He didn't, but I did! At first I found it hard to get used to obeying orders but I enjoyed the camaraderie of basic training. I trained as an avionics technician, gaining a BTEC level 3 in Aerospace Systems Studies. My job was maintaining Tornado GR4s, Canberras, and VC10s. I worked my way up to senior NCO, and I'm now working in the RAF's career service.

Chapter 4

Royal Navy

The Royal Navy defends the seas around our coasts and helps to police the world's oceans to stop international drug smuggling and terrorism. Like the other armed services, the Royal Navy also brings aid to countries devastated by wars and natural disasters. The Navy is not just a fleet of highly specialized fighting ships and submarines. It has its own fleet of fighter aircraft and helicopters, the Fleet Air Arm, and its own crack troops (most highly trained soldiers), the Royal Marines. Some staff work in shore bases around the world, providing the rest of the service with technical and administrative support.

below: *This Royal Navy ship is decked out with flags to celebrate the 200-year anniversary of the Battle of Trafalgar.*

Many careers to choose from

Ships, planes, the Royal Marines, and shore bases – each offer many careers with different starting qualifications. You can join the Navy with no qualifications or you can join with GCSEs/S-grades, A-levels or Highers, and even with a university degree or professional training. How do you decide which is for you? Having read this chapter, the next step is to visit your local Armed Forces Careers Office (AFCO).

At the AFCO you can ask a member of staff any questions about the Navy before filling out a questionnaire. If you want to join as a **rating**, you will be tested in English language, mathematics, **reasoning**, and mechanical comprehension. If you pass these tests you will be invited back for an interview with a careers officer, a pre-joining fitness test, and a medical examination.

If you want to join as an officer, you need to have five GCSEs or S-grades including English and Maths, and the equivalent of three A-levels (D, D, and E) or three Highers (grade C). The selection process takes place over 2 days at the Admiralty Interview Board. It involves written tests, leadership tasks, a planning exercise, and an interview, as well as fitness and medical tests. Royal Marines have to complete the Potential Officers Course at the Commando Training Centre Royal Marines in Devon before attending the Admiralty Interview Board.

Get acquainted

If you want to join as a rating and would like to find out more, you can attend a Royal Navy Acquaint Centre Course on HMS *Caledonia* in Scotland. Here you will get a taste of life in the Navy and help in deciding which career to choose.

Get ahead!

Browse the Royal Navy's website (www.royal-navy.mod.uk) to find out all you can about the Royal Navy. It also gives information on individual careers and the qualifications needed for each. You can join the Sea Cadets or the Combined Cadet Force, if there is one in your area.

Worried about seasickness?

Don't worry – everyone gets seasick from time to time. You may feel queasy at first but you will soon get your sea legs. After several weeks at sea, your main problem will be adjusting to firm ground for the first few days back on shore!

Training

Once you have been selected as a rating you will begin basic training at HMS *Raleigh* in Cornwall. Basic training lasts 8 weeks and, once you have signed the enrolment form, you must stay for at least 4 weeks. During basic training you will learn about the Royal Navy, first aid, and fire-fighting. You will also learn about a warship and its weapons systems and practise parade-ground drills.

Improving your fitness is an important part of basic training for all recruits. By the time you have finished basic training you should be able to run 2.4 km (1.5 miles) in less than 12 minutes 20 seconds if you are male, and less than 14 minutes 35 seconds if you are female.

below: *This Royal Navy recruit is practising camouflage techniques.*

Officers

To train as an officer, you go to Britannia Royal Naval College in Dartmouth, Devon. The training takes between 28 and 49 weeks. The first 14 weeks are spent developing leadership and communication skills and learning how to handle a boat on the River Dart. You then spend 7 weeks on an operational warship before returning to college for strategic studies and more academic work. This is followed by another stint on a warship to learn about all the different branches of the Navy, before continuing professional training in a particular area of the service.

Royal Marines

The Royal Marine Commandos are an **amphibious** fighting force. They can launch an assault by land, sea or air at short notice anywhere in the world – in mountains, deserts, jungles, or the Arctic. They are often the soldiers who spearhead an attack, the first front-line troops to engage in battle. Training at the Commando Training Centre in Lympstone, Devon, lasts 32 weeks and, if you are fit enough and determined enough, you should be successful.

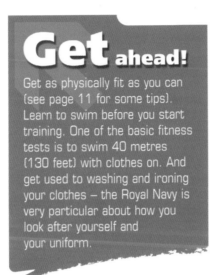

Get ahead!

Get as physically fit as you can (see page 11 for some tips). Learn to swim before you start training. One of the basic fitness tests is to swim 40 metres (130 feet) with clothes on. And get used to washing and ironing your clothes – the Royal Navy is very particular about how you look after yourself and your uniform.

above: *Being able to swim is essential if you are thinking of joining the Royal Navy.*

KNOW YOUR SHIPS

Ship	Main function	No. in ship's company
Aircraft carrier	Carries fighter jets and helicopters	685 + 386 aircrew
Assault ship	Carries troops and helicopters for fighting on land	325 or 285
Destroyer	Provides anti-air defence to protect groups of ships	287
Frigate	Anti-submarine and multi-purpose fighting ships	250 or 185
Submarine	Carries torpedoes and/or missiles	135 or 130
Minehunter	Keeps Britain's coasts free of mines	45 or 34
Patrol boat	Protects Britain's fishing fleet and offshore gas and oil rigs	45 or 30

Careers in the Royal Navy

Careers in the Royal Navy are more varied than in any of the other services. In the Navy you can work below the sea as a diver or submariner, on the sea in a ship, in the air in the Fleet Air Arm, or as a Royal Marine Commando. For most jobs, ratings do not need academic qualifications; instead you have to pass selection tests and interviews to be accepted for particular jobs.

Surface ships

The Royal Navy has more than 70 surface ships. Some of them are shown in the box on page 27. All carry weapons and have state-of-the-art technology and communications systems, plus engineers, technicians, and IT specialists to operate them. In addition they employ administrative staff, chefs, and healthcare specialists – doctors, nurses, and dentists.

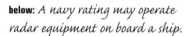

below: *A navy rating may operate radar equipment on board a ship.*

Submarines

The Royal Navy has 15 nuclear-powered submarines, some of which carry nuclear weapons. Submarines stay at sea for many weeks at a time, so to join a submarine you have to be able to live in a confined space for long periods. Jobs for ratings include operating the machinery and systems and collecting information on which the captain and officers base their decisions.

MEN ONLY

Not all jobs in the Royal Navy are open to women. Royal Marine Commandos fight on the front line and so, in keeping with the **Geneva Convention**, are not open to women. Women cannot work on submarines or do mine-clearance diving because these could harm their health.

above: *These aircraft handlers are refuelling an aircraft on the flight deck of an aircraft carrier.*

Fleet Air Arm

The naval air stations are at Yeovilton in Somerset and Culdrose in Cornwall. The Harrier is the Navy's **fixed-wing** fighter jet – it can take off and land on a short airstrip, often on the deck of an aircraft carrier. Jobs on board aircraft carriers and on air stations include maintaining the aircraft and helicopters and managing them during take-off and landing.

CASE STUDY

Dawn is a leading writer in the Navy.

*I joined the Navy when I was 21. The training on HMS Raleigh was hard work for me, particularly the physical fitness, but finishing it gave me such a sense of pride. My job is as a leading **writer** dealing with pay, leave requests, and travel. I work on shore bases and on ships – I spent 2 and a half years at sea on the aircraft carrier HMS Invincible. What I enjoy most about the Navy is all the friends I've made and the places I've been, particularly the 3 months I spent in the US on a training exercise. I am already a middle manager and aim to become a petty officer.*

Chapter 5

The police force

Police work involves a lot more than chasing and arresting suspected criminals. As a police officer you have to be able to communicate well in many different situations: talking to members of the public, writing up crime reports, and presenting evidence in court. Police officers also spend a lot of time trying to prevent crime and educating the public on how to avoid crime.

below: *The police force is keen to recruit people from all ethnic groups.*

Police forces

Each region in Britain has its own police force. You do not need any specific academic qualifications to become a police officer, but you do need to have a good general education to pass the selection process. Each force has an equal opportunities policy – they employ both women and men and, particularly in large cities, are keen to recruit people from different ethnic groups.

Applying to become a police officer

The first step is to fill out an application form. It will be checked and, if your application is accepted, you will be sent an information pack and invited to an Assessment Centre. Read the information pack carefully – it explains exactly what will happen at the centre. Some police forces even offer to help you to prepare for the assessment process.

The assessment process involves written tests, role plays, and an interview. One of the written tests, Verbal Logical Reasoning, assesses how well you can analyse facts and evidence. The role plays give you the chance to show how well you communicate and handle different kinds of situations.

If your tests and interview are successful, you will have a medical test, an eye test, and a fitness test. Take note – most people who fail to get in to the police force do so because they are not fit enough. You do not have to be as fit as people applying for the armed forces, but you do need to have a good level of general fitness. The police will also do various security checks to see, for example, whether you have a criminal record, and other background checks. All being well, you will be sent a letter offering you a place.

below: *Police divers have to search rivers and other waters for evidence.*

Get ahead!

It will help your application if you can show that you are a responsible member of the community. You could become a police cadet, for example, learn first aid or help out at a youth club.

DO YOU QUALIFY?

To join the police force you need to:
◎ be at least 18
◎ be physically fit
◎ meet the required eyesight standards
◎ be a UK citizen, a Commonwealth citizen, or member of the **EU** or **EEA**, or a foreign national with unrestricted residency.
How tall you are is not a factor!

Training

Anything can happen to police officers on the beat. They need to be able to handle a wide range of situations, from administering emergency first aid, or helping an elderly person who cannot remember where they live, to stopping a fight, helping victims and witnesses of crime, and arresting suspect criminals.

Recruit training

Each police force trains its own recruits, either at its headquarters or at its own training centres. Training of recruits varies from force to force, but includes lectures in the classroom and practical exercises. Together they teach you all the skills you need to be an effective police officer, particularly the ability to make quick decisions, communicate with the public, and treat them fairly. Hendon Police Training College in North London trains recruits for London's Metropolitan Police Service and has its own police station and a mock courtroom where recruits can practise for the real thing.

Get ahead!

Visit the website
www.police-information.co.uk or
www.policecouldyou.co.uk to find
out about courses and home
learning that will help you at all
stages of your training.

During recruit training you will learn a lot about the law and about correct police procedures. As a police officer you must be above suspicion, so you will be expected to maintain the highest professional standards and levels of **integrity**. Training also teaches you self-defence and emergency first aid and improves your physical fitness. You have to pass every part of the course to carry on to the next stage as a **probationer**.

Probationer training

Training doesn't stop when you become a probationer. For the next 2 years you will pound the beat as an independent police officer, putting everything you have learned into practice. At the same time you will be carefully assessed and supervised by a training officer.

CASE STUDY

Will Taylor, a police officer, explains why he joined the police.

I decided to join the police because of a personal experience. I was attacked and mugged by three youths, but luckily a police car happened to drive by about 30 seconds later, so I flagged it down. They caught all three of the muggers and arrested them. It made such a difference to me that I wanted to do the same for someone else. I completed my 2 years as a probationer a few months ago. One of the really good things about the police is the range of specialisms. When I'm ready, I'd like to train as a dog handler.

above: *Probationary officers work with experienced officers when they are on the beat.*

A choice of careers

After 2 years on patrol as a probationary officer, what then? Many police officers decide to stay on the beat and perhaps be promoted through the ranks to sergeant, inspector, and so on. Other officers decide to train and specialize in one particular aspect of policing.

Specialist branches vary from region to region but are likely to include rapid response officers, scene of crime officers, dog handlers, neighbourhood police officers, traffic police, and a firearms unit. Competition for specialist jobs is fierce and you need to show an aptitude for a particular specialism before you will be chosen to train in it.

Dealing with crime

Rapid response officers are usually the first on the scene of an incident. Officers are trained to assess situations fast and take appropriate action. If firearms are involved, they may call in the firearms unit. They are trained to use weapons, but only as a last resort. Scene of crime officers take photographs and fingerprints, and collect **forensic evidence**, such as hairs, clothing fibres, and blood samples. The evidence is then examined in a laboratory by forensic scientists who check **DNA** and fingerprints and look for incriminating chemicals.

CID

The Criminal Investigation Department (CID) is staffed by detectives. They investigate serious crimes, including murder, assault, rape, **fraud**, and robbery. They work closely with scene of crime officers and forensic scientists, and use the huge police database to check details of known suspects. Experienced CID officers may go on to work in the Fraud Squad, the Drug Squad or the Crime Squad.

above: *Police horses are trained to remain calm whatever the situation.*

Other specialisms

Traffic police make our roads safer by trying to prevent motoring offences as well as catching and prosecuting law-breakers. Most forces have a helicopter and air support unit, which they use to track people, get officers to crime scenes quickly, and to rescue casualties.

Most forces also have dog handlers, who each work with a particular dog. A dog's sense of smell is much better than a human's, so dogs are useful for sniffing out drugs and explosives. Many forces also have specialist units for dealing with crime within the family. Some officers focus on child protection and others on domestic violence, but they are all trained to deal sensitively with very vulnerable people.

Neighbourhood policing

Neighbourhood police officers specialize in preventing crime. They get to know people in a particular community and are often the first to receive information about crimes. Police community support officers work alongside police officers, although they do not have as many powers as police officers. Neighbourhood policing means working mainly out of doors and spending a lot of time on your feet, walking around. Police officers and community support officers usually work in pairs.

Neighbourhood police officers

Neighbourhood officers work closely with community leaders and local community groups. Some officers may specialize in **youth intervention**. They visit schools as part of the school curriculum. They may also set up anti-bullying services and advise children on how to avoid dangerous or confrontational situations.

above: *Police community support officers get to know people in the community.*

Police community support officers

Police Community Support Officers (PCSOs) provide a visible presence and help to reassure people who are worried about crime. They can give out some fixed penalty notices and can detain suspects until a police officer arrives.

To qualify as a PCSO you need to fulfil the same conditions as a police officer. You have to fill in an application form and complete an assessment process similar to that used for police officers. You do not need academic qualifications, but you need to be able to write up reports. More importantly, you need to be good at dealing with the public and making quick, confident decisions. The training is shorter than for police officers and covers the law, first aid, and patrolling skills.

Parking enforcement

Making sure that drivers had parked correctly used to be the job of traffic wardens and was a responsibility of the police force. Now, however, local authorities (town councils and county councils) are taking over responsibility for parking. Parking in the wrong place stops the traffic flowing well, so drivers who do not keep to the rules are given fixed penalty fines. Traffic wardens, also called parking attendants, check whether motorists have paid the correct parking fees. Parking offences are not crimes, but dealing with angry motorists is not easy and is sometimes dangerous.

You do not need to have academic qualifications to be a parking attendant but you do need to be able to speak and write English. You also have to be calm and tactful and good at handling difficult situations. Your training will help you do this.

Chapter 6

Fire and rescue service

The fire and rescue service deals not only with the serious job of fire-fighting but with much more besides. Fire-fighters are called out whenever there is a major incident, such as a rail or air crash, a major road accident, or a terrorist bomb. They are also called out to more minor accidents, such as people stuck in a lift, or to a flood in a basement. As well as answering emergency calls, fire-fighters educate the public about fire safety and clean and maintain their fire engines and equipment.

Get ahead!

If you are aged between 13 and 19, find out if your local fire service runs a LIFE course (LIFE stands for Local Intervention Fire Education). The course lasts a week, during which experienced fire-fighters teach you some fire-fighting skills. You can also help to prepare yourself for the selection tests by doing a **BTEC** qualification in Public Services. Even better, City of Wolverhampton College run a Fire Service Pre-Recruitment Access Course.

Organization

Britain does not have a national fire service. Instead, there are 47 regional fire and rescue services. Although there are some differences, they all select and train new recruits in much the same way. Most fire and rescue services employ retained fire-fighters as well as full-time fire-fighters. Retained fire-fighters are men and women who live or work near the fire station. They may be builders, shop-keepers, typists or technicians, for example, but, when the "bleeper" goes, they drop what they are doing and become part of the fire-fighting team.

Qualities of a good fire-fighter

You have to be at least 18 years old and physically fit to become a fire-fighter, and you need to have the right qualities. Do you have a good head for heights? You need to if you want to be a fire-fighter! You need determination and courage and you have to be able to think clearly and act quickly in confusing circumstances. You also need good stamina so that you can keep working in, for example, smoke-filled buildings.

But the fire service does much more than fire-fighting. A large part of their work involves educating the community about fire safety, so fire-fighters also need good communication skills. You do not, however, need to have academic qualifications – the only way to get into the fire service is to pass the selection test.

COMMUNITY FIRE SAFETY

The aim of community fire safety is to reduce the risk of fire. Fire-fighters educate the public about smoke alarms and tell them how to avoid kitchen fires and fires caused by smoking cigarettes. They inspect hotels and public buildings to make sure they reach fire safety standards.

above: *These fire-fighters are rescuing people trapped in a car after a road accident.*

The selection process

The fire and rescue services insist that there are no short cuts to getting in. Everyone, whether they are university graduates or have no academic qualifications, has to go through the same selection process. You have to apply to a particular fire and rescue service and it will only take you on if it has a vacancy. Vacancies are hotly contested!

How do I apply?

The first step is to contact a fire and rescue service and, if they are recruiting, they will send you an application pack. Make sure you fill in the application form correctly – see page 48 for tips on how to fill in application forms. Provided your application form is accepted, you will be invited to a training centre for selection tests. These include written tests and physical fitness tests. The tests are followed up by an interview and a medical test.

Get ahead!

The best way to do well in the selection process is to prepare well. Browse the website www.fireservice.co.uk – it tells you what to expect and is full of tips and hints. Read the application pack carefully and make sure you are physically fit before you apply. Before your interview find out everything you can about the fire and rescue service and the particular job you are applying for.

Written tests

The written tests assess how well you can take in information and how accurately you can remember it. For the numerical tests you have to calculate numbers in your head. Observation tests assess how well you can observe and weigh up a situation. Mechanical tests find out how practical and mechanically minded you are. Several books have been written on different types of tests so that you can practise them in advance (see page 53).

New selection tests are brought in from time to time. Read your selection pack carefully!

Fitness tests

The physical tests are challenging, mentally as well as physically. The actual tests vary from one region to another but will probably include the "bleeb test". For this you have to run 20 metres (65 feet) back and forth on a track to the sound of a bleep. You hear a bleep when you start and a bleep at the end of each 20 metres. The problem is the bleeps get closer together, so that the run gets harder, not easier. You can find out more about the bleep test on the website *www.fireservice.co.uk*.

Other physical tests include running out hoses, for example running out six 25-metre (82-foot) hoses in 8 minutes, and climbing ladders – to make sure that you are comfortable with heights. To see if you can work in confined spaces, you will have to find your way in the dark through a crawling alley wearing full breathing gear.

left: *These recruits are learning how to pitch a ladder.*

Training

Basic training for full-time fire-fighters takes place at the fire and rescue service and lasts from 13 to 20 weeks. It is hard work – about 70 per cent of it is practical and 30 per cent is theoretical – and you are constantly assessed. Retained fire-fighters do a basic training course followed by sessions at their local stations at the weekends and in the evenings.

above: *Fire-fighters on a training exercise.*

The first phase

Basic training is also called Phase 1 training. First, you learn fire-fighting skills, such as handling hoses, pumps and ladders. You also learn about health and safety – although fire-fighters work in dangerous conditions they know how to avoid unnecessary risks and hazards.

Then you are taught how to use breathing apparatus and how to rescue people from confined places. You learn how to deal with incidents such as traffic accidents, air, and rail crashes. Such incidents often involve using powerful cutting equipment to rescue people, administering first aid, and dealing with serious trauma injuries.

Phase 2 training

Phase 2 covers the first two years of your career in the fire station. You will be regularly assessed as you put what you have learned in Phase 1 into practice. You also add to your theoretical knowledge through further learning modules.

Further prospects

New equipment and procedures are constantly being introduced, so training and assessment continue throughout your career. You can also apply for promotion or for specialist training in, for example, community fire protection, driving a fire engine, or operating a turntable ladder. As a child you may have dreamed of driving a flashing, wailing fire engine through busy streets – the reality takes many months of special training!

CASE STUDY

Elisabeth explains why she became a fire-fighter.

I wanted to join the fire service because I'm an active, sporty sort of person and I wanted to help the community. The selection and training were physically challenging but, with the help of the trainers and the other people on the course, I was able to achieve all the required standards. Fire-fighting is not just about strength, though – it's also about good communication skills, relaying information, and calming people involved in an incident. Every day and every incident is slightly different – I'm always learning something new. Best of all, I am making a real difference to other people's lives.

KNOW YOUR ENGINES

Fire appliance	What it does
Pump ladder	Carries crew, hoses, ladder, and equipment
Turntable ladder platform	Has extra-long extendable ladder for reaching people in high buildings, but no hoses or equipment
Foam tender	Specialist vehicle for dealing with chemical fires
Incident Response Unit	Carries special equipment, such as decontamination equipment, for dealing with terrorist incidents

Chapter 7

Other civilian services

Apart from the police and fire service – the main civilian forces – there are smaller forces who are concerned with the security of the nation. They include customs and excise, immigration, and the prison service. They also include coastguards and Trinity House, who look after the safety of ships around the coasts. Most coastguard stations are in remote areas and are staffed by people who have retired from the Royal Navy.

Customs and excise

The main work of customs and excise officers is to stop smuggling, particularly drugs and other illegal items. Smugglers are also people who try to avoid paying duty or tax on, for example, imported cigarettes. Customs officers work closely with the police and most of their work goes on behind the scenes. You may, however, have seen a customs officer at an international airport, searching someone's luggage.

Excise officers inspect import companies and **distilleries** to make sure that the correct duty is being paid, while VAT officers check whether companies are paying the correct levels of Value Added Tax (VAT) to the Government.

To join the service as a junior manager, you need to have five GCSEs (grades A–C) or five S-grades (grades 1–3) and two A-levels, Highers or the equivalent. If you have at least two GCSEs (grades A–C) or two S-grades (grades 1–3) you can apply to join the service lower down and work your way up. If you are accepted, you will be trained and may eventually be promoted to customs officer or excise officer.

above: *Customs officers often use dogs to sniff out illegal items at international airports.*

Immigration

Immigration officers work at airports, ports, and at the Channel Tunnel. Their job is to make sure that everyone who enters the country has the correct passport, **visas** or work permits. They have to assess whether people are telling the truth about their reasons for coming to Britain. Immigration officers have to be well organized and good at keeping written records. To apply to be an immigration officer you need to have the equivalent of two A-levels, but you can join as an immigration assistant with five GCSEs (grades A–C). You must be a UK national and have lived in Britain for the last 5 years. Your basic training will be at Heathrow or Gatwick airports or at Dover, and you must be willing to work in different parts of the country.

Get ahead!

To be an immigration officer you need to have a GCSE in English language and it helps if you can speak another language.

The prison service

Prison officers supervise people who have broken the law and have been sent to prison or who are in prison awaiting trial. They also supervise young offenders in remand centres and other institutions. Their job is not just to keep prisoners in order, but to support and care for them, too. You have to do shift work, often through the night, and spend most of the time indoors, inside a prison.

Qualities of a good prison officer

The prison service is looking for people who can work in a disciplined environment, with many rules and regulations, and, at the same time, empathize with prisoners. You have to be able to keep order, on the one hand, and win prisoners' trust and confidence, on the other hand. You have to be committed to helping people who are in a difficult situation.

Qualifications and training

Scotland, England and Wales, and Northern Ireland each have their own prison service with their own rules about age and qualifications. In England you have to pass an entry test and interview, while in Scotland you must have five S-grades (grades 1–3) or have worked for three years managing people.

Basic training lasts several weeks. It includes role playing in various situations and specialist training for those who are going to work with young people. The training continues for the whole of the first year, during which time you are supervised and supported by an experienced member of staff.

DO YOU QUALIFY?

To join the prison service in England and Wales, you need to:
◎ be at least 18 and a half years old
◎ be a British or Commonwealth citizen or a member of the EU
◎ have been living in Britain for at least the last three years
◎ pass medical, eye, and fitness tests
◎ not belong to any organization that the prison service considers to be racist.

Specialist jobs

There are several different specialist jobs within prisons. Some involve working directly with prisoners, such as a nurse or instructor. Instructors teach trade skills, such as woodwork, engineering, and tailoring. Other officers specialize in jobs to do with running the prison, such as administration, catering, driving, gardening, and so on.

above: *Prison officers can specialize in gardening and work in the prison garden.*

What have you already done that is relevant to the service or job you are applying for? Have you, for example, ever had to take responsibility, or give or take orders? Are you a school prefect or leader of a youth group? Why do you want to join the service? What are you hoping to get out of it?

Application forms

Your application form is the first impression that the recruitment officer or employer will have of you. Read the form carefully and think about your answers before you fill it in. It is a good idea to photocopy the blank form and practise on it. Once you are satisfied with all your answers, copy them carefully onto the proper form.

Interviews

The best way to do well at an interview is to prepare well. Find out everything you can about the force you are interested in. If you are applying for one of the armed forces, read up about any ongoing military situation, such as Iraq, and find out about the current situation in Northern Ireland. All the armed and civilian forces are committed to treating everyone equally, whatever their gender, religion or race. Make sure you know the policy and what it means, especially if you are applying for the police.

Good luck!

DOS AND DON'TS FOR INTERVIEWS

- Arrive early. Being late makes a very bad impression.
- Dress smartly and look business-like. Don't wear the kind of clothes you would wear for a night out with your friends.
- For the armed forces, cut your hair short if you are male.
- Don't wear body piercings.
- Make sure your shoes and finger nails are clean.
- Be confident. Look the interviewer in the eye and answer questions clearly.

Examples of careers in the armed forces

BRITISH ARMY

Examples of jobs for privates	Main qualifications needed to get in	Some of the qualifications you can achieve	Possible regiments
COMBAT			
men only: Infantry Soldier; Tank Crew; **men or women:** Gunner	No academic qualifications	Full driving licence; NVQs in, for example, training and development	Any of 32 infantry battalions; Royal Armoured Corps
COMBAT SUPPORT			
Engineering			
Signals Electrician; Vehicle Mechanic; Heating and Plumbing Engineer; Combat Engineer	GCSEs in Maths, Science, and English or equivalent trades qualifications	LGV trailer licence; City & Guilds engineering qualifications; BTEC diploma in engineering	Royal Corps of Signals; Royal Electrical and Mechanical Engineers; Royal Engineers
IT and Communications			
Signals Electrician; Radio Systems Operator; Electronics Technician; Operator Military Intelligence	GCSEs in Maths, Science, and English or equivalent NVQ and BTEC qualifications	City & Guilds Engineering qualifications; BTEC National Certificate in Engineering	Royal Corps of Signals; Royal Engineers; Intelligence Corps
Logistics			
Technical Storeperson; Chef; Driver; Postal Courier Operator	Some jobs require no academic qualifications; others require GCSEs in English and Maths	NVQ in Food Preparation and Cooking; Department of Transport licences; NVQs	Royal Logistic Corps; Royal Artillery; Army Air Corps; Royal Corps of Signals
SERVICES			
Administration			
Military Clerk	GCSEs in English and Maths	NVQ in Business Administration	Adjutant General's Corps
Healthcare			
Healthcare Assistant; Veterinary Technician	Good education; GCSEs; appropriate BTEC or nursing qualifications	Recognized professional qualifications	Royal Army Medical Corps; Royal Army Veterinary Corps
Specialist			
Dog Trainer; Musician; Royal Military Police	Qualifications vary with job	Qualifications recognized by civilian equivalents	Royal Army Veterinary Corps; Corps of Army Music

ROYAL AIR FORCE

Examples of jobs for aircrew and trades	Main qualifications needed to get in	Some of the qualifications you can achieve	Civilian equivalent
AIRCREW			
Weapons Systems Operator	5 GCSEs/S-grades, including English Language, Maths, and Physics	BTEC and other qualifications recognized by civilian aviation companies	Navigation specialist or other specialist job
ENGINEER			
Aircraft Technician; General Technician; Weapon Technician	3 GCSEs/S-grades in Maths, English Language and an approved Science or Technology subject	City & Guilds Aeronautical Engineering; Engineering Maintenance	Electrical or mechanical engineering technician
IT and COMMUNICATIONS			
Air Traffic Control Assistant; Aerospace Systems Operator; Flight Operations Assistant	2 GCSEs/S-grades in English Language and Maths; none	Apprenticeship in Information Technology	Air Traffic Controller
Communications and Information Systems Specialist	3 GCSEs/S-grades in English Language, Maths, and Science	Advanced Apprenticeship	Telecommunications Technician
ADMINISTRATION			
Personnel Administrator; Physical Training Instructor; Mechanical Transport Driver	none; GCSE/S-grades in English Language; none	NVQ in Business Administration; Coaching; NVQ in Handling Air Passengers	Office manager; Sports Coach; Courier
Catering			
Chef; Air Steward	None	Apprenticeship in Hospitality	Chef, Caterer; Air Steward, Food Manager
Healthcare			
Medical Assistant; Dental Technician	none; BTEC in Dental Technology	Recognized qualifications in Medical Assistance	Paramedic; Dental Surgery Assistant
Security			
Regiment Gunner; RAF Police; Fire-fighter	None	NVQ in Security; Advanced Apprenticeship in Firefighting	Security Guard, Police Officer, Fire-Fighter

ROYAL NAVY

Examples of jobs for ratings	Qualifications needed

WARFARE

Communications and Information Specialist working with communications equipment;	GCSEs/S-grades
Mine Warfare Specialist operating sonar equipment;	GCSEs/S-grades
Mine Clearance Diver	none

SUBMARINE

Warfare Rating (Submariner);	none
Engineering Technician (Marine Engineering Submariner);	GCSEs/S-grades
Chef	none

FLEET AIR ARM

Naval Airman (Aircraft Handler) preparing and controlling the flight deck;	none
Naval Airman (Survival Equipment) involved in training aircrew in survival techniques	none

ENGINEERING

Air Engineering Technician maintaining fixed-wing aircraft and helicopters;	none
Engineering Technician (Weapons Engineering) responsible for weapons, radars, and sonars;	GCSEs/S-grades
Engineering Technician (Marine Engineering) responsible for the ships' engines	GCSEs/S-grades

ADMINISTRATION

Stores Accountant;	none
Steward;	none
Chef;	none
Writer responsible for administrative and clerical duties	none

HEALTHCARE

Medical Assistant;	none
Dental Surgery Assistant;	GCSEs/S-grades
Naval Nurse	GCSEs/S-grades

Websites

General

◎ how2become Ltd (*www.how2become.co.uk*) – This website has tips about applying to join each of the armed and civilian forces. It also sells CDs that contain lots of information on each of the forces, including their selection processes, tests, and interview questions.

◎ Learndirect (*www.learndirectadvice.co.uk/helpwithyourcareer/jobprofiles/ profiles/*) – Go to "Security Services and Uniformed" for job profiles for the armed and civilian forces.

British Army

◎ The Army Cadet Force (*www.armycadets.com*) – This is the official ACF website.

◎ The British Army (*www.army.mod.uk*) – This is the official website for the Army. It includes profiles of the different jobs. It also allows you to chat to a recruitment officer online and to download a copy of the Army's fitness programme.

◎ My camouflage (*www.mycamouflage.co.uk*) – This is a website for 13 to 17-year-olds, with games and information about Army life and about sponsorship by the Army for further education.

Royal Air Force

◎ Air Cadet Organization (*www.aircadets.org*) – This is the official ACO website, with information about target shooting, flying, and other ACO activities.

◎ Royal Air Force (*www.raf.mod.uk*) – This is the official website for the RAF, providing information about the aircraft, training, and different jobs available. It also has links to information about sponsorship.

◎ Royal Air Force Careers (*www.rafcareers.com*) – Go to this RAF website for more information on careers: the qualifications you need to apply, the qualifications you can gain, and much more.

Royal Navy

◎ Royal Navy (*www.royal-navy.mod.uk*) – This is the official website of the Royal Navy, with information about the ships and submarines, Fleet Air Arm, and Royal Marines. You will find everything you could want to know about the Royal Navy on this site.

◎ Sea Cadets (*www.sea-cadets.org*) – This is the official website for the Sea Cadets.

Police

◎ Metropolitan Police (*www.metcareers.co.uk*) – This is the official website for London's Metropolitan Police.

◎ Police careers (*www.policecouldyou.co.uk*) – This website has information to help you decide whether you could be a police officer and how to apply.

◎ Police information (*www.policeinformation.co.uk/Docs/policetrainingcourses/directory/index.html*) – This website tells you about police training courses and courses that will help you pass the police selection test.

◎ UK Police Service (*www.police.uk*) – You can access all the regional police forces and non-geographical forces from this official site.

Fire and Rescue service

◎ Apprenticeships (*www.apprenticeships.org.uk/youngpeople/*) – This website tells you about apprenticeships that are available for the fire service.

◎ Fire service information (*www.fireservice.co.uk*) – This is an unofficial but useful website for the fire service. Go to "Recruitment" for information and tips on the application process.

Books

General

◎ Corfield, Rebecca. *Preparing Your Own CV* (Kogan Page, 2003)
◎ Corfield, Rebecca. *Successful Interview Skills* (Kogan Page, 2006)
◎ Parkinson, Mark. *How to Master Psychometric Testing* (Kogan Page, 2004)
◎ Smith, Heidi. *How to Pass Numerical Reasoning Tests* (Kogan Page, 2003)
◎ Tolley, Harry and Ken Thomas. *How to Pass Verbal Reasoning Tests* (Kogan Page, 2000)

Armed and civilian forces

◎ Bryon, Mike. *How to Pass the Firefighter Selection Process* (Kogan Page, 2004)
◎ Higgins, Nick. *Real Life Guide to The Armed Forces* (Trotman, 2004)
◎ Hindle, Fiona. *Getting into The Armed Forces* (Trotman, 2002)
◎ Pilgrim, Dee. *Real Life Guide to The Police Force* (Trotman, 2004)
◎ Tolley, Catherine, Ken Thomas and Harry Tolley. *How to Pass the New Police Selection System* (Kogan Page, 2004)

amphibious able to go on land and in water

aptitude test test that measures whether someone has the ability to learn particular skills

avionics electronics used in aviation

BTEC Business and Technician Education Council. The qualifications it awards include the Higher National Certificate (HNC) and Higher National Diploma (HND).

commissioned officer officer whose rank is from second lieutenant to field marshall. Commissioned officers are of higher rank than non-commissioned officers (NCOs) and they have to have completed commissioned officer training.

customs and excise Government department that collects taxes on imports and exports and certain other goods, such as alcohol

destitute without a home, food or enough money to support yourself

distilleries factories where strong alcoholic drinks, such as whisky, are made

DNA deoxyribonucleic acid, the complex molecule that carries genetic information in living things

drills repeated exercises used in training

EEA European Economic Area. Its members are the 25 countries of the European Union plus Norway, Iceland, and Liechtenstein.

EU European Union, a group of 25 European countries that have agreed to work more closely together to maintain a peaceful and financially successful Europe

fieldcraft skills needed to operate and survive on active service

fixed wing type of aircraft wing that does not move

forensic evidence objects or substances that relate to a crime. Forensic evidence includes fingerprints, poisons found in the stomach, and drops of blood.

fraud obtaining money by deception

front line zone of battle where two sides in a war confront each other

Geneva Convention agreement accepted by most countries that sets standards of reasonable treatment of victims of war, prisoners of war, and troops

halal meat from an animal that has been prepared according to Muslim law

initiative ability to make your own decisions

integrity honesty and keeping to high moral standards

kosher meat that has been prepared according to Jewish law

logistics successful organization of a large and complex operation

Modern Apprenticeship Scottish apprenticeship, lasts for 4 years

National Vocational Qualification (NVQ) in England and Wales, a work-related, competence-based qualification that shows you have the knowledge and skills to do a job effectively. NVQs represent standards that are recognized by employers throughout the UK.

non-commissioned officer (NCO), officer in the Army whose rank is from lance corporal to staff sergeant or colour sergeant; petty officer in the Royal Navy

operations action that involves several people working together

platoon group of about 28 soldiers within a regiment or corps

probationer recently qualified person in their first year or two of service

promotion being raised to a higher rank or more responsible job

radar system that uses radio waves to detect the position of aircraft, ships or objects that are too far away to be seen

rating sailor in the Royal Navy who is not a commissioned officer

reasoning ability to think logically about facts and reach a conclusion

reconnaissance observation of enemy territory or military forces to obtain information

regiment large group of soldiers

sonar system for detecting objects or ships under the sea using sound waves

squadron group of aircraft, ships or troops of soldiers

terrain area of land, often with particular natural features, such as a desert or mountain

visa entry in a passport showing that the holder of the passport is allowed to enter the country and the length of time they are allowed to stay

writer Royal Navy term for someone who works in administration

youth intervention work undertaken with young people to reduce the possibility of their becoming criminals or victims of crime